Sucess
BLUEPRINT

Timeless Principles to Enable You to Identify & Accomplish True Success & Fulfilment in All Areas of Life

Dr Sylvia Forchap-Likambi

Success Blueprint:

Timeless Principles to Enable You to Identify & Accomplish True Success & Fulfilment in All Areas of Life

New, in-depth, and expanded edition of Principles of Resolution with new and significant insight into identity, goals, purpose, and true success.

Copyright ©2020 by Dr Sylvia Forchap-Likambi

ISBN-13: 978-1-913266-98-1

All rights reserved. No part of this book may be reproduced or transmitted in any form or by any means, electronic or mechanical, including photocopying, recording, or by an information storage and retrieval system – except by a reviewer who may quote brief passages in a review to be printed in a magazine or newspaper – without permission in writing from the copyright owner.

Other Books by the Author:

A Father's Tender and Compassionate Love

ISBN 10: 1479772887/ ISBN 13: 9781479772889
ISBN 10: 1479772879 ISBN/ 13: 9781479772872

Seven Powerful Strategies for Overcoming Life Challenges

ISBN-13: 978-1975669584
ISBN-10: 1975669584

Principles of Resolution – A Practical Step-by-Step Guide to Enable You Identify, Set & Accomplish Your Goals

ISBN 10: 1543063780
ISBN13:9781543063783

TABLE OF CONTENTS

DEDICATION i
Acknowledgements iii
PREFACE v
INTRODUCTION 1
CHAPTER ONE : IDENTITY 7
    The Devastating Effect of Ignorance 14
    13 Fundamental Questions to Help You Identify Who You Are and What You Need to Be Fulfilled and Successful 17
    Four Fundamental Questions to Enable You to Identify and Establish Your Goals and Achieve Success 22
    Practical Examples to Assist in Writing Your Goals 24
CHAPTER TWO : MOTIVATION 27
    A Guide to Establishing Your Motivation and Drive for Success ... 34
    Unhealthy Motivation to Avoid When Setting Your Goals 35
    Healthy and Commendable Motivation to Consider When Setting Your Goals 37
    Healthy and Compelling Motivation is Fundamental and Indispensable for Your Success and Fulfilment 40
    Sustainable and Long-Lasting Benefits of a Healthy & Compelling Motivation 46
CHAPTER THREE : AMBITION 49
    A Guide to Establish How Ambitious You Are 50
    A Guide to Establish How Ambitious Your Goals Are 51
    A Guide to Enable You to Identify and Avoid Unambitious Goals . 52
CHAPTER FOUR : REALISATION 55

A Step-by-Step Guide to Enable You Bring Your Goal into Realisation 58
CHAPTER FIVE : TIME...................................... **63**
CHAPTER SIX : ACTION **71**
CHAPTER SEVEN : REST..................................**79**
CHAPTER EIGHT : A Guide to Enable You to Identify Key Areas in Your Life Where You Could Effectively Set Desired Goals **85**
CONCLUSION.. **101**
AUTHOR'S BIOGRAPHY **113**

DEDICATION

This book is dedicated, with love, to all those who are yearning to live a fulfilled, purposeful, and successful life and would love to start planning and preparing for it now.

Acknowledgements

My profound gratitude goes to my darling and wonderful husband, Mike—for your endless support and love towards me... ensuring that I continue to live a purposeful and fulfilled life and become all that I was created to be.

To my amazing and magnificent children and love— Latoya, Caleb, and Destiny; For enabling me to experience the exceptional joy and fulfilment that come with motherhood, I could never have asked for any better! Thank you for making me the tremendously successful and fulfilled mum and role model/ mentor that I am today.

To my beautiful family, beloved friends, pastors, colleagues, loved ones, and the millions of men and women I have been privileged to work with and serve globally —thank you for enabling me to fulfil my unique purpose of existence and experience the deep sense of satisfaction and fulfilment that comes with living a purposeful life... Living each day to the fullest of my potential and gloriously!

Finally, endless gratitude to my Heavenly Father and Creator, for the magnificent gift of life, purpose, and wisdom!

PREFACE

It was the 27th of December 2016, just two days after Christmas, and the final days of 2016... I was lying down on the couch in my living room, relaxing, and watching my three little children play and sing together as they explored and talked about their Christmas gifts with much excitement and joy. I could overhear the two older ones giggle with excitement about their wishes for that Christmas coming true... I could also hear them talk about what they would love to have as their Christmas presents the following year.

As they discussed their wishes for the following Christmas, I could hear them speak with so much certainty and conviction, without any doubt whatsoever—as if it all depended on them and must surely come to pass! For a moment, I smiled, saying to myself, *How I wish life was like this ...having all your wishes and heart's desires come true simply by asking for them.* I carried on with this inner self-talk. *If they only knew the reality of life ...if they only knew that you do not always get what you desire or wish for in life then they wouldn't be speaking with such assurance and confidence—as though it is all under their control and guaranteed.* Then, suddenly, I realised that my thoughts were contrary to the fundamental beliefs that I hold ... and also contradictory to the same lesson and philosophy I teach them daily. This philosophy guides them to be positive and hopeful at all times, believing that all things are possible through Christ who strengthens us and that whatever they ask it shall be given unto them—provided it is not for selfish reasons or detrimental and harmful to them and/or towards others. In fact, Mathew 7:7 is our mantra; it says, "Ask and it will be given to you; seek and you will find; knock and the door will be opened to you." My children literally take this quotation word for word and often wonder why they ask sometimes but do not receive...

Upon reflecting on my own philosophy and the above scripture, I quickly hushed myself and redirected my focus and thoughts towards *"the power of staying positive and hopeful."* I have personally experienced this power numerous times in my life and family and seen so many people I work with also experience it in such a profound state—over and over again.

However, before I could finish my self-talk, I could hear my son saying to my daughter, "Aaahhh ... Mummy wouldn't let you have an iPhone... She says you are still too young to have one ... and remember you got the Blackberry last Christmas!" Then my daughter was like,

"But I can't even call anyone with it and it is old-fashioned!" She goes on, this time even more confident and firm in her tone than before. "Anyway, I can buy it myself you know... I will publish more books, save some money, and get an iPhone for myself!"

By this time, my entire attention was focused on them and their baby sister, who just enjoyed her toys without really knowing the difference. To her, it was just another toy and another day. Without saying a word, I kept listening and avoiding any eye contact or any gesture that would distract and hence interrupt them. I could see my son was super excited and happy for his sister. In his state of enthusiasm, he suddenly said, "Aaahhh... I am also going to write and publish loads of books, so I can have much money and buy whatever I desire and also help some of the poor children who have very little or no money at all ... yes!"

He screamed with excitement then ran towards me and gave me a big and affectionate hug. He looked me in the eyes and said, "Yes, yes, Mummy! Latoya and I are going to write loads of books and have so much money so we will be able to buy whatever we want and also help poor children who have no money!"

Looking at my little boy, and the excitement he had about his new dream, I felt really proud and privileged to be his mum. I am also very proud of my daughter, who is already a published author and is currently working on her third book (during the time of this incident, she was working on her second book). One other thing I noticed, which is very obvious, is the fact that the excitement he showed while talking about publishing his books and getting the money to acquire his heart's desires was very different and much more profound than that which he previously expressed while talking about having his Christmas wishes coming true!

At this moment, my daughter also joined in and hugged me with so much excitement and determination in her voice—as she validated what her brother just told me a couple of minutes earlier. Then she took it a step further ... and this really astonished me!

She called her little brother. "Caleb, come on... Come and let's go upstairs and get our computers and start writing straight away; we do not have much time before it's Christmas again, you know." At this point, I couldn't stop smiling. They then gave me loads of hugs and hurriedly disappeared into the corridor, and upstairs they went ... with their baby sister running after them.

I was indeed very pleased and proud of them! I pondered and pondered, saying to myself, *If only I knew what they now know when I was their age... I would certainly be a multimillionaire today.*

I know you may be wondering, *But what do they know that you didn't know? What was the difference between you and them when you were younger?*

Now, before I can respond to the above questions and tell you exactly what they know that I didn't know then, and hence the fundamental difference between my upbringing and theirs, I would first of all like to draw your attention to some key elements and differences that I noticed as I watched them and listened to them speak.

First of all, I noticed the excitement and sense of satisfaction they expressed as a result of receiving their desired gifts and requests for that Christmas.

Secondly, I observed that the confidence and assurance they both exhibited as they talked about their wishes and desires for the following Christmas was also very obvious ... until the iPhone was mentioned.

Thirdly, and most interestingly, I immediately became aware of a renewed enthusiasm, excitement, and greater confidence in my daughter as she found a solution to the setback that would potentially hinder her from having her heart's desire for an iPhone fulfilled. I then asked myself, *But why this renewed enthusiasm and greater confidence?*

Suddenly, I began having some profound revelation, which then inspired me to begin the process of writing this book straight away so it could be available in the New Year—as everyone prepared to walk into a new era of their life and hence identify and set their New Year's resolutions based on what they would like to achieve in the New Year and beyond...

Here is the revelation, which is exactly what I never knew as a child—however, my children, then aged seven and 10 years respectively, seemed to have grasped and mastered it at such tender ages. It became even more obvious to me that my children were very aware of the fact that their dreams and goals had more power than their wishes ... and that if they dedicated some time and put in the necessary effort, then the former would certainly come into realisation.

A dream could be defined as a cherished aspiration, ambition, or ideal; while a goal is a desired result or possible outcome that a person or a system envisions, plans, and commits to achieve. On the other hand, a wish is simply a strong desire for something to happen with no effort to make it happen or become a reality! For this reason, it is often said, "If wishes were horses, then beggars would ride..."

In fact, there is a great difference between wishes, dreams, and goals... Wishes are the things you strongly desire or want, however without having to commit to do something in order for it to happen. In order words, wishes are not dependent on your commitment or efforts but rather on external factors and elements, which are always changing and quite uncertain. It is very evident that as a child I was not aware of these fundamental differences between the three, and consequently how they affected us and determined the probability and/or certainty with which we achieved our heart's desires and were fulfilled.

While growing up, it was sufficient for my siblings and me to simply present our wish lists to our parents and then wait for them to become reality on Christmas Day or on some other special occasions, such as birthdays. From one Christmas and New Year to the other, all we ever did was write down our Christmas and New Year lists, which were often filled with our wishes and hearts' desires for the year and expected to become a reality on Christmas day—in effect, brought to us by the famous *"Father Christmas"*.

Contrary to my daughter and son, we never thought then of ever taking it a step or two further... Hence, our wishes were never transformed into dreams and eventually goals ... and we totally depended and relied on our parents for these wishes to come true! Notwithstanding, we were always confident that they would certainly come true, though we weren't exactly sure of what specific ones in our lists would become reality and which would remain forever wishes and eventually fade away with time...

In fact, I now understand why their excitement was profound the moment they spoke about committing to write their own books and raise the money they needed for their Christmas gifts... At this point, they no longer had just wishes, which are less dependent on them and without any commitment on their part in making them come true. Conversely, their wishes were dependent on external forces/sources, which in this case were us—their parents. Nonetheless, because they know and trust us, they were confident that almost all of their Christmas wishes would become reality, except for the iPhone...

Nevertheless, as soon as their wishes were transformed into dreams, and eventually backed by a definite goal and action plan, their excitement and confidence were doubled ... if not tripled. Why? They were more assured it would become a reality as it did not depend on others or external factors but greatly depended on them – their efforts and their ability and willingness to commit and make it happen – and they were indeed committed to making it happen.

In fact, they did not only commit, but in such a short space of time, they had come up with the necessary strategy and plan required to make this achievable ... and immediately set out to implement the first steps necessary to make their dream a definite goal and tangible reality! This signified that they were aware of the fact that success is deliberate and intentional; and the outcome was a deep sense of satisfaction and fulfillment.

While I had all this revelation, I pondered even more, visualising images of some of the highly successful people in the world and trying to figure out what truly sets them apart from the ordinary and average people and makes them so successful in life. In my quest for an answer, I immediately thought about a very common and persistent trait or characteristic that is often observed in the lives of each and every one of these extremely successful individuals, which is their inherent ability to have well-defined goals and plans for their lives thoroughly mapped out—a success blueprint. They then live their lives focusing on accomplishing and fulfilling such goals and plans. We all know that when we fail to plan in life, we automatically plan to fail.

SUCCESS BLUEPRINT

Over the years, I have worked with several individuals from various background and culture who find it very hard to identify what they really want in life and hence their ideal goals and heart's desires/life purpose and consequently what will make them truly successful and happy. Some have told me that they don't even know what they want or need to do in order to be successful. Others have testified that they feel like they are not living the life they desire and deserve to live and are unhappy with their lives, though not knowing exactly what they desire—they feel a great void and unrest within.

On the other hand, there is a small category of those who know exactly what they want, but lack the willpower, drive, and guidance to either initiate or stay persistent and consistent and not give up along the way. Some have set amazing goals and resolutions every now and again but lack the motivation and consistency to drive them forward and succeed.

This book represents a very practical manual and blueprint, full of well tested and proven life principles and laws of nature, indispensable for identifying, planning, preparing for and achieving success and fulfillment in every area of life. Therefore, as I write this simple and practical guide book/manual, I do so with great excitement and enthusiasm—with the intention of guiding and enabling many ordinary people to identify what true success means to them and then plan, prepare, and achieve true success in every area of their lives.

Dr Sylvia Forchap Likambi

Hence, this book is designed and written to serve as blueprint for success, to guide, equip, and empower you with the tools, resources, and fundamental principles required to embark on an inspirational journey of transformation, purpose, and fulfilment—as you transit into a new era and new year of your life. It is a privilege and honour to address and impact you in a positive way through this piece of work—full of simple and very practical tools and strategies and a clear road map to explore, navigate, and implement in your life with immediate effect.

Transiting into a new year and new era, I was inspired to write the first edition of this timeless book and communicate this message to you—as a tool to inspire and motivate you and many others out there to make the deliberate choices and decisions to resolve unsettled issues in your past and present lives and turn over to a brand-new page and chapter of your lives...

Of note, when I talk about a new year or new era of your life, I want you to know that this could be any season and time in your life, and not necessarily a new calendar year. It may mean different things to different people, and what is important is that you relate to it based on what it means to you and to your life and transformation. To you it may be a new year of life following another birthday, to another it may be a new beginning following a very tragic past or loss, and to another it may be a brand-new chapter and year of their life, etc. What ever a new year may mean to you, I would like to create a mutual point of reference by connecting that and every other meaning given to it by other readers to a new beginning—a new calendar year. I have deliberately chosen this as a reference point because each time we transit into a new calendar year almost everyone seeks to begin all over again or transit into a completely new year and phase of their lives and hence make the necessary plans and set New Year's resolutions and goals to guide them through this new phase and year of their lives. Every New Year seems to bring with it a renewed hope and enthusiasm to many ... a sense of assurance that the new year will somehow or definitely be better and full of many opportunities than the previous—therefore there is a lot of optimism and excitement!

Like me, I am sure you are also excited to embrace and witness another year of life—full of new/endless possibilities and opportunities for you and me, waiting to be explored, exploited, and maximised...

The best thing I love about a new year is that, like all new things, it is amazingly NEW! I mean "BRAND NEW". It has never existed before... It is original, authentic and simply NEW—No stories told ... no experiences lived ... no traces left ... no songs sung, etc. It is absolutely new and it is expected that you and I will fill it up with the stories we want to tell, the experiences we want to live, the traces we want to leave behind, the songs we want to sing, and so on. Let's ride on then into this new adventure and life and live it to the fullest—it's a new year and a new era...

Consequently, we must consciously and deliberately create the stories, experiences, traces, songs, etc., we want to be part of during this new year and season and coexist with it! So, let's set our intentions for the season!

Yes, you sure heard me well—it's up to you and me to personally make that decision and choice to imagine, design, and co-create whatever we want to be a part of the new and live this new opportunity and life just the way you and I would want and love it to be lived ... no permissions, no excuses, no apologies... We must sow into the new year and season all that which we would love and expect to reap. Now, let's pick up a pen and a notebook, sit back, relax, and begin planning and mapping out our journey and strategy to a successful and fulfilled life—our success blueprint, unique and bespoke to us.

In the meantime, I will take this unique opportunity to wish you a wonderful and glorious ride into a new era and season of your life ... an era of true success and fulfilment in every area of your life; full of abundant health, wealth, love, peace, optimal relationships, profound joy, and happiness.

Before I proceed any further, I would like to take some time in the next chapter to explore the origin of New Year's resolutions and the unchanging traditions of setting goals and resolutions following the dawn of another calendar year—a new year. This will give us insight into the original concept of goal setting and New Year's resolutions.

INTRODUCTION

> *"For last year's words belong to last year's language. And next year's words await another voice. And to make an end is to make a beginning."*
>
> - T.S. Eliot

The concept of New Year's resolutions dates back to some 4,000 years ago, when ancient Babylonians held celebrations in honour of the new year, which for them began in mid-March, when the crops were planted, rather than January. During such celebrations, which lasted for 12 days, they crowned a new king or reaffirmed their loyalty to the reigning king. In addition, they also made promises to the gods to return any borrowed objects and pay their debts. Such promises are considered the predecessors of our New Year's resolutions.

Dr Sylvia Forchap Likambi

The ancient Romans also carried out a similar practice, following the establishment of January 1st as the beginning of the new year by Emperor Julius Caesar. During this time, the Romans offered sacrifices to their God Janus, the two-faced god, and made promises to be of good conduct for the coming year. Furthermore, early Christians traditionally celebrated the first day of the newyear thinking about their past mistakes and resolving to do and be better in the future.

For me, the beginning of a new year is always a time of profound reflection and meditation—on how my life has been throughout the year and during the final days leading to the end of an era in my life and the beginning of a new one. I take an inventory of my life and evaluate whether it has been successful and purposeful and if I am still on track and working hard and deliberately towards fulfilling my purpose. I take with me the lessons learnt from both past successes and failures with the aim of implementing them in the new year and improving in every area of my life.

I always use this amazing moment as an opportunity to review and restore my plans and vision for my life – while taking some time out to refresh and revive so I can be able to bounce back stronger and better than ever before – and I am guessing and hoping this is the same or similar for you.

I'm certain that by the time you are reading this book, you must have already begun your journey. Consequently,

I would like to draw your attention to the fact that prior to any significant life journey rest/reflection and planning are prerequisites. Therefore, you must take some time out of your busy schedule to be still and reflect upon your life and identify and establish the goals you would love to set and accomplish as you step into a new era of your life.

As you read this book, I would encourage you to examine how your life has been in the past and what it is in your life that you would love to improve and make better henceforth.

In life, the one thing that is constant is change. You know why? I guess it is because life is so kind, fair, and gentle to us, such that it gives us endless opportunities to start all over again and let go of our past ... all the time! Yes, I mean all the time! It gives us immense possibilities and platforms to sow again, reap again, be born again, and be renewed, restored, etc.

It also gives us millions of opportunities not to conform and be trapped in what WAS and IS, nor in our past and the old, but to be constantly transformed by the renewal of our minds at every given instant and moment, such that our thoughts are continually renewed, and hence our words and actions; processes which eventually and automatically result in the divine renewal and transformation of our lives and destinies—giving us the ultimate chance to eventually live the life we were created and destined to live and enjoy life in abundance.

Dr Sylvia Forchap Likambi

A new year, just like a new day, is a new year for everyone. It could be envisaged as a new and fertile soil given unto you to start afresh, sow afresh. It is the same soil provided unto every one—no one has sowed in this soil yet and no one has reaped from it yet. So all you really need is YOU and YOUR SEED in order to take advantage of the endless opportunities and gifts entrapped within the NEW SOIL and NEW YEAR waiting for you to exploit and unleash them!

Do not worry about your past failures or unsuccessful harvest of the past... Take full responsibility and advantage of the NOW; it has got nothing to do with the PAST or OLD. In the same manner that light and darkness cannot coexist, Old and New cannot coexist and you must not synthesize an OLD-NEW or NEW-OLD life or situation ... it is either one or the other! The choice is yours to make. In the same manner, "no one puts new wine into old wineskins. For the old skins would burst from the pressure, spilling the wine and ruining the skins. New wine is stored in new wineskins so that both are preserved." Matthew 9:17

Therefore, based on what you would expect and love to reap you get the specific seed type and sow that particular seed. You can't sow tomatoes and expect to reap mangoes; in the same way, you can't expect to reap oranges and yet choose to sow tomatoes then blame the soil or the season and the neighbours for not being able to reap the oranges you expected and loved!

It is reassuring to see that, each time we move into a new year, many people start looking for new ways of life and hence make New Year's resolutions for the purposes of improving their lives and becoming better persons. It is a period when most people thrive to resolve something they haven't been able to resolve before or set a new target for themselves and bring about solutions and improvements in many areas of their lives ... and that is where the term "Resolution" steps forth.

The amazing thing I love about a new year is the endless opportunities and platform it provides to us to start afresh and these endless opportunities are for everyone—so we may recreate the life we so desire and envisage for ourselves. It symbolises a brand-new page/chapter of our life.

Imagine a blank sheet of paper or a blank screen given unto you to fill up with whatever you choose. You are given the power and authority to write down whatever you want to write on it—what will you write? Some people already know exactly what to write on the blank screen or page, while for others there is still uncertainty and a lack of clarity around what to actually write...

One thing is certain; if you write nothing, then you will have nothing in the season of harvest. However, someone has to write down something on the new sheet of paper—with each new day representing a brand-new sheet. Therefore, if you do not write something down or fill it up, someone else or life circumstances will ... and I am sure you do not want this to happen.

Here is a clue to help you identify what to write: you might have missed something or messed up in the past and would love to make up for this in the new year. You might want to leave behind some of the fears of the previous year that were holding you back and embrace the mental strength and courage to walk boldly and fearlessly into the new year, determined like never before.

In this regard, I will be taking you through a journey of empowerment and transformation, during which I will be equipping you with the tools and resources needed to enable you to access the power, authority, and influence within you and transform your life for good as you step into a new year and era of your life.

Without taking much of your time, I will be providing you with my seven core/fundamental laws and principles (success blueprint) that you will need to examine and start implementing in your life straight away – without delay – in order to identify, set, and accomplish your goals and heart's desires. They will enable you to establish what true success means to you, ensure you remain focused and on track for living a fulfilled and purposeful life. Now, let's take a look at these laws and fundamental principles in the subsequent chapters of this guide.

CHAPTER ONE

IDENTITY

> *"When you do not know who you are or what you want in life, there is a great tendency for you to eventually settle for a mediocre life! Therefore, to live an all-fulfilling and exceptional life, it is paramount that you go back to the basics of self-identification."*

The first blueprint or rule of thumb to apply is the law of identity. The Oxford English Dictionary defines identity as the characteristics determining who or what a person or thing is.

When faced with the question, "Who are you?" what is your usual response? We live in a world where many simply do not know who they truly are or why they even exist in the first place. Identity crises are a huge problem in our society today, resulting in so many health conditions and complications—and worst of all suicide!

Many cannot even stand the look of their image in the mirror as it appears to be a complete stranger, unknown to them! Others go on living another person's life or, even worse, the identity bestowed on them by society or other people without ever understanding who they truly are, what brings them a deep sense of fulfillment and satisfaction or why they exist!

I strongly believe that knowledge is power, (or, more accurately, potential power) and I cannot emphasize this enough. In Hosea 4:6, it says my "people perish; my people are destroyed as a result of a lack of knowledge." However, I must place emphasis on the fact that knowledge of the truth is what is powerful and it brings about genuine transformation and liberation. "And you will know the truth, and the truth will set you free." John 8:32

Notwithstanding, simply having access to knowledge of the truth is not sufficient to bring about real transformation. It is the effective application of the knowledge acquired that makes all the difference and determines whether or not you will be successful and fulfilled ... and this is called wisdom! Wisdom can be defined as one's ability to discern and pass judgment between what is wrong and right, and what is good and bad, and effectively apply the knowledge aquired where and when relevant.

Hence, when you know the truth about yourself – who you are; where you have come from; why you are here on Earth; what you can do/your full potential; where you are going to; and why – and live that truthfully and wholeheartedly, then you can truly start experiencing true freedom and success—and that is what this manuscript is all about.

Now, you might be thinking, *But what is this truth you are talking of? What do you mean by knowing the truth about yourself?* It is worth mentioning that knowledge is simply information. Therefore, the information could either be false or true, depending on the source and content. However, what is actually required in order to experience true transformation and liberation is not just any type of information (knowledge) but knowledge of the truth—hence wisdom.

Consequently, as you go through the chapters of this book/manual, it is my utmost heart's desire and wish that you extract the appropriate knowledge/information that is valuable and relevant to you and subsequently apply it to those specific areas of relevance in your life as you journey through this new year and new era of your life. In view of that, your principal goal should be to seek knowledge of the truth and, above all, wisdom.

Dr Sylvia Forchap Likambi

I assure you that the easiest and fastest way to keep a people enslaved and unsuccessful is to deprive them of knowledge of the truth; therefore, you cannot afford not to know the truth about yourself, and, hence, your authentic identity. Becoming ignorant of this truth leaves you as an easy target and prey for enslavement, exploitation, and abuse, and worst of all, one becomes a slave and prisoner in one's own mind!

For example, when we look back into the past, it would have probably been easier for people to be enslaved than it is today because they lacked knowledge/access to knowledge of the truth about themselves/who they truly were and authentically represented. They lacked knowledge of the great and untapped potential and resources that were entrapped within them. They lacked knowledge of their inherent ability to shape and transform their lives, families, nations, and continent as a whole. The lack of such vital knowledge must have predisposed them to easily conform, and settle for mediocrity and worse.

The same thing is happening in our society today and taking a slightly different facet ... very close to our homes. Today, many, especially women, are disadvantaged, oppressed, enslaved and constantly being exploited as objects of pleasure, abuse, etc. simply as a result of the fact that they lack indepth knowledge of who they truly are. They lack knowledge of the immense potential and abilities entrapped within them to change and shape their lives, stories, and history. Too often, they are entrapped and enslaved in their own minds—battling with identity crises and insecurities.

Of note, your identity is simply those traits and qualities that make you different from others, hence it is very unique to you. Literally speaking, it is what sets you apart from me and everyone else on Earth. In the same way, my identity sets me apart from you and everyone out there. For this reason, we have identity (ID) cards, such as passports, driver's licenses, etc., through which we are identified and distinguished; and no two people can have the same ID card/s.

It would be helpful for you to know that prior to your birth and existence your identity had already been established and subsequently concealed within you and in your genetic code (DNA). Humanly speaking, your DNA actually has some very unique and specific codes within it – yet to be decoded – and it is largely responsible for those unique traits and characteristics that distinguish you from others, setting you apart and making you unique. Overall, it is responsible for providing an indication of who you are and will eventually become. Of note, not even a child has the same DNA as the mother or father; neither do identical twins—even though we call them *"identical twins."*

I hereby urge you to arise, wake up, step out, and identify/redefine who you are; why you exist; where you are heading to and what success means to you and eventually stand out from the crowd! In doing so, you will identify and map out your own destiny and success blueprint, and you are capable of planning for it in advance and achieving immense success and fulfilment.

Above all else, seek wisdom and make the decision, here and now, to apply it in your life—as you embark on your own transformational journey and path to success. This is the time—your time; your time is here and it is now! There is no better place than here, and no better time than now, to begin this journey of yours—it is a brand-new opportunity and chance—like none you have ever experienced before... *"Carpe Diem"*! (Seize the day!) Again, there is absolutely no better time than now, nor better place than here ... it is very timely—while you read this wonderful guide and blueprint take advantage and act now!

It is your responsibility and duty to be at the forefront of identifying and redefining your authentic identity and ideal life. In essence, you must take full responsibility for your life and be the one to define and set those goals that are indispensable to enable you become the change you want to see in your life, family, and world and achieve success and fulfillment in all areas of your life and career. You can do this only if you are willing to. Stop waiting for people, society, situations, life circumstances, and the pressures of life to define who you are and what you want and need in life in order to be "successful" and determine the type of life you should live, and, consequently, the types of goals you must set for yourself and accomplish.

I have a burning desire within me to speak specifically to you as you read this book and stir within your spirit a great desire for a new revelation of who you truly are—as a very unique individual. In this way, you may be able to identify, set, and accomplish your life goals and fulfill your purpose of existence and experience maximum success and satisfaction.

It is very obvious that, when you do not know who you are, you will certainly never know what you really need/want in life and you will (without any doubt) eventually settle for mediocrity, accepting and validating this lifestyle as the norm. In addition, you will inevitably abuse/misuse yourself by not maximising and fully exploiting the endless and great potential that lies within you—dormant, untapped, and unknown. If you are unaware of your greatest strengths, you will definitely let others undermine you and toss you around. Regrettably, you will also let them abuse/misuse and/or exploit you—consciously or unconsciously. Now, what do I mean by the above statement?

Basically, abuse comes from the fusion or two words; abnormal and use. Hence, the abnormal use of an object or an individual, and/or resource, results in abuse of that object, individual, and/or resource, respectively. When you abuse an individual or an object, it implies that you use that individual or object contrary to its original purpose or intent of creation or manufacture. Consequently, not having a good grasp and knowledge of your true identity, worth, and hence purpose of existence, makes abuse/self-abuse or misuse/exploitation inevitable.

Of note, there are two fundamental reasons why we abuse ourselves or let others abuse us. The first reason is ignorance – ignorance of our identity, and purpose – and therefore our worth will inevitably lead to abuse! The second reason is misuse of power/authority and/or exploitation. In this case, people use their free will and the power conferred to them to either oppress us or exploit our ignorance and/or vulnerability. The latter, unfortunately, is quite heartbreaking and manipulative and one of the key reasons why you cannot afford to have a misconception about your identity or be ignorant about your true identity.

You simply cannot afford to become vulnerable and easy prey for exploitation, which may lead to a self-identification crisis—and a huge negative consequence for your overall health and well-being and ability to succeed. Having said this, is ignorance an excuse? Not at all! Ignorance is deadly, ignorance is costly, and, above all, ignorance destroys lives and robs destinies—it is much more costly than knowledge.

The Devastating Effect of Ignorance

In order to bring to light the huge negative implications that are associated with a lack of knowledge (ignorance) of your identity, we will now examine a few practical examples that highlight the fatal implications of ignorance. Let's imagine that you are in the process of getting your driver's license, but you do not know the purpose of the traffic lights on the road. As a result, you are ignorant and unaware of the fact that when the traffic lights are green, it signifies that you can drive on and when they are red, it signifies you must stop.

Now, let's analyse the consequences of ignorance from the above example. If you were to drive on when the lights are red, two things may happen: first of all, you would be accountable, liable, and fined—and you could also be convicted. The most interesting thing is that it doesn't matter whether you are aware of the law or not. Irrespective of whether you are ignorant of the law or not, you will still be fined—as it is against the law to go through the traffic lights when they are on red. Secondly, you might have an accident and destroy your life as well as the lives of others, simply as a result of going through the traffic lights while they were on red!

Hence, ignorance is no excuse; neither does it exempt you from the law and the consequences of your actions! Moreover, the worst thing about being ignorant of your true identity and worth is the fact that it predisposes you not only to an abuser who lacks the knowledge of who you are/your purpose but also to self-sabotage.

Let's look at another very practical and straightforward example... Imagine a three-month-old baby who does not know the purpose and function of a mobile phone. What do you think she will do if I hand over my smartphone to her for an hour or two?

The first thing she is very likely to do is to put it straight into her mouth and try to bite it/eat it. She is also very likely to throw it/hit it on the ground and take pleasure in hearing it bang on the floor and then pick it up again and try to eat it or throw it again...

In doing all of the above, does it signify that this cute little three-month-old baby is mean or bad/unkind? Absolutely no! She is merely ignorant of the purpose of the smartphone, and hence she abuses it out of ignorance! If I also did not know the purpose of the phone, I would certainly let her continue to play with it and destroy it; however, because I know the purpose of the phone, I will eventually stop her, and take it away from her. In fact, I would not even allow her to have the phone and play with it in the first place.

This is very similar to what happens to us when we do not know the purpose of our life, we let other people abuse us and, worst of all, we abuse ourselves and are unable to maximize our full potential—because we are not even aware of the great potential that is entrapped within us. As a result, we will not be able to tap the greatness within us and use it to fulfill our purpose on Earth and, hence, become successful.

Being ignorant of your true identity and worth is therefore detrimental to your success, as is not exploiting and maximising your full potential—because it makes room for others to exploit and maximize them on your behalf, to fulfill their own hearts' desires and dreams … leaving you void, unsuccessful, and unfulfilled.

Consequently, to enable you to identify and establish who you are and what goals or problems you would love to resolve , what true success means to you, in your life and in the world – which will henceforth bring you profound satisfaction and success – I have put forth a series of very

SUCCESS BLUEPRINT

simple and straightforward questions for you to explore, reflect on, and respond to.

Your responses to these questions will serve as a guide to support you in setting the most significant and fulfilling goals in your life that will result in great accomplishment and fulfillment/success.

13 Fundamental Questions to Help You Identify Who You Are and What You Need to Be Fulfilled and Successful

By clearly responding to the following questions you will be able to have an in-depth knowledge of yourself and of what really matters to you and brings you joy and fulfillment.

1) Who are you? How do you identify yourself?

_____
_____
_____
_____
_____

2) Where have you come from? What is your source or origin?

_____
_____
_____
_____
_____

3) Why are you here? Why do you exist on planet Earth?

_____
_____
_____
_____
_____

4) What are the fundamental beliefs you hold about yourself and why?

_____
_____
_____
_____
_____

5) What are your core values? What are the principles that you will never compromise on?

_____
_____
_____
_____

6) What are the things that excite you most in life? What are your passions?

_____
_____
_____
_____

7) What brings you fulfilment and satisfaction?

_____
_____
_____
_____

8) What does being successful mean to you?

_____
_____
_____
_____

9) What is your purpose for living/why are you living?

_____
_____
_____
_____

10) What are your greatest strengths?

_____
_____
_____
_____

11) What are your greatest weaknesses?

_____
_____
_____
_____

12) What is your vision? Where are you going to? Where do you see yourself in the next 20–30 years?

_____
_____
_____
_____

13) What can you do? What do you have in your hands?

_____
_____
_____
_____

Take as much time as you need to go through the questions and come out with definite answers. Reflect on them...

If in any doubt, speak to loved ones who know you very well. Seek a life coach or mentor to enable you to unleash your authentic identity and establish your core foundation before proceeding. It will be helpful to write down your answers before proceeding to the next chapters of this book—but if that's not possible, then read on... The step-by-step guide will provide you with more enlightenment and clarity to help you identify who you are and what you want...

It is crucial and fundamental that you are able to identify and establish who you are, why you are here, what success and fulfillment mean to you and, eventually, what your vision is and what you can do—which will be based on who you are and what brings you ultimate fulfilment and satisfaction. Once done, you should be able to identify and establish what is important to you and what you want to achieve and resolve in your life—thus providing you with a guide and road map to clarify and facilitate the process of setting, accomplishing, and fulfilling your desired goals.

Four Fundamental Questions to Enable You to Identify and Establish Your Goals and Achieve Success

Now, having identified and established who you are and what is important to you – as an individual, a woman, a man, or a group, etc. – I want you to respond to the following questions to help you identify the specific goals that you want to set for yourself.

1) What problem/s do you want to solve in your life/family/community? Be very specific and succinct.

_____
_____
_____
_____
_____

2) What do you want to resolve in your life now and in the next 10 years?

_____
_____
_____
_____
_____

3) What are the results you would like to accomplish?

SUCCESS BLUEPRINT

_____
_____
_____
_____

4) What solutions do you want to bring about this year and in the next 10 years?

_____
_____
_____
_____

At this stage, once you have identified and established what you actually want to resolve and accomplish and your priorities for this new year and the future, you should take some time to reflect on them—write them down on a blank sheet of paper or in a notebook. You should write down all of your identified goals and vision for the year and where you would like to see yourself by the end of the year and, if possible, in the next 10–20 years from now—in no particular order. In writing them down, you solidify them and make them concrete.

> *"Write the vision; make it plain on tablets, so he may run who reads it."*
>
> **- Habakkuk 2:2**

On the other hand, if you have already identified and established who you are and what you want, what success means to you and your specific goals in the past, then now is the time for you to re-identify/re-evaluate and reflect on them to ensure that you are working towards fulfilling them. You need to establish whether or not you are still on track to fulfilling your purpose and vision and identify and set strategies/principles to keep you motivated, passionate, and tenacious at all times—most especially in challenging and difficult times.

Once you have written down all the goals that you would love to accomplish, you can move on and focus on what is most important to you at this moment in time; allocate numbers to them in order of significance—with the most significant taking priority and having the number 1 assigned to it and so on.

Do not work in terms of urgency – which is the main reason why planning in advance is crucially important – as this eliminates unnecessary stress and pressure. Since you have enough time now, you should prioritise your work and execute it in order of importance and significance—working initially on the goals that are more important to you and will bring you maximum satisfaction and, in turn, have positive effects on the other less significant goals and your productivity and energy boost.

Practical Examples to Assist in Writing Your Goals

In writing down specific goals, you should employ these core principles in order to be motivated to act now and remain motivated until your goal is accomplished. During this initial stage of goal setting, you must be very specific/direct. For example, you could say, "I want to achieve A, B, C by the end of February or by the end of the year." Clearly write down your goals and make them solid.

Let's consider a simple example to guide you on how you could effectively write your identified and established goals. Let's look at the area of health and well-being—you must be very specific about the problem you have identified, established, and would love to resolve in this area of your life now and in the future.. Let's assume your problem is overweight or obesity and you want to solve this problem and achieve a healthier weight and lifestyle.

On this basis, you need to be very specific about what a healthier weight and lifestyle is. For example, let's assume you want to lose 30 kg from your current weight, which is 100 kg, and therefore arrive at a final weight of 70 kg and also develop a more active lifestyle, which involves walking for 15 minutes a day. You should write your goal in this format: My goal is to walk for 15 minutes every day and weigh 70 kg by the end of August. This is a very specific goal, with a very precise instruction delivered to your mind, which will now set out to respond and execute your command—motivating you to take action and keep acting until the desired results are achieved.

> *"Knowing others is intelligence; knowing yourself is true wisdom. Mastering others is strength; mastering yourself is true power."*
>
> **- Lao Tzu**

CHAPTER TWO

MOTIVATION

> "The greatest independent factor that drives success and fulfilment is intrinsic motivation."

The second blueprint or rule of thumb/principle to implement is the law of motivation, which states that, "The greatest independent factor that drives success and fulfilment is intrinsic motivation." In its simplicity, motivation is defined in the Oxford English Dictionary as "a reason or reasons for acting or behaving in a particular way." You should be able to establish the reason/s why you have chosen the specific set of goals above and not others—you should be able to clearly state the motive/s for setting and wanting to accomplish these goals and become successful.

There are two types of motivation—intrinsic motivation, which comes from within you and is associated with what drives you internally into taking action, and extrinsic motivation, which is associated with an external factor or incentive. Notably, external motivation can only be effective if the intrinsic component is present. In other words, being externally driven to take action in response to an incentive/appealing offer or reward will not necessarily move you into acting; if there is no ulterior motive or reason within you to qualify why you should act in the first place?

Let's consider a simple and straightforward example. Imagine you are at home, relaxed and reading a newspaper, when you suddenly come across this very appealing and promising job offer as an executive marketing director in a global company. The job offers a prestigious salary, a complimentary luxury car, and loads of free international travel opportunities, which include flying first class and staying in some of the most prestigious hotels in the world. For an instant, you are carried away by your imagination... Notwithstanding, you quickly get back into your reality and continue reading the newspaper, slowing putting aside the thoughts of the highly appealing job offer you just read about and thinking to yourself, *How I wish my work would offer me such benefits and luxuries.* Yet you take no action and carry on reading the newspaper.

Suddenly, a still little voice within you then reminds you, *"Remember you have got a great job you very much love and enjoy, and you look forward to every single day because it brings you great satisfaction and fulfillment, even though the financial reward and incentives are not excessive."*

Almost instantly, you drift away again, though this time you are thinking about your work—why you do it, your love and commitment towards it, your staff and customers, the value you add to their lives and those of their loved ones. Subsequently, you whisper, "I truly love my job, and for nothing in the world could I ever give up all the fulfillment and satisfaction it brings me."

Hence, in spite of all the sumptuous rewards and incentives promised by the advertised job, you are not internally motivated and driven to take action and apply for the job as there is no intrinsic motive for you to do so. Your intrinsic motives are key determinants of every action you take in life.

> *"For every action in life, there is an underlying intrinsic motivation, whether we are aware of this or not—it is therefore in our best interest to become conscious of this fact."*
>
> **- Dr Sylvia Forchap-Likambi.**

Dr Sylvia Forchap Likambi

Everything we do in life has a driving motive behind it, and that's where the word motivation comes from. One of the definitions of motivation that I really love and use quite often is this: motivation is the process that initiates, guides, and maintains goal-oriented behaviours. The first thing to take note of in this definition is the fact that if there is no goal then there is no motivation. In addition, you should note that it is a process and not a static reference point. It is not an endpoint either but rather a continuous and dynamic process. Finally, from the definition, you will also notice that there are three major components associated with motivation, and these are: activation, management, and sustainability.

The activation process involves all those elements and factors that inspire and drive you to make the crucial decision to eventually take the bold step towards initiating that goal-orientated behaviour—this state is fundamentally intrinsically driven. The management process involves all those key components/characteristics required in order to remain focused and disciplined and stay on the right track of accomplishing your goals—irrespective of the obvious obstacles and setbacks you may encounter along the way. In effect, it requires the willpower to act and keep acting even when you don't feel like doing so or when you come across a great obstacle or challenge along your path. This stage requires persistence, tenacity, endurance, and continued effort in the direction of your goal, even though obstacles may exist.

Finally, the process of sustainability ensures that your behaviour/actions are continuous/uninterrupted and sustainable towards a definite purpose—until your desired goal/outcome is achieved and a successful lifestyle established and guaranteed. This stage ensures that you develop a new lifestyle that empowers you and enables you to maintain and not lose your recent achievement and to become accustomed to this lifestyle and remain successful.

Thus, it is fundamental that you understand that there is a motive behind every action you take in life, whether you are aware of this or not. Ignorance does not and will never be a substitute for truth! Thus, the earlier you become aware of the motives behind why you do things and establish that, the better and more successful and fulfilled you will become. On the other hand, if you fail to establish this, someone or society will do this for you ... and when this becomes the case, you are doomed to conform to the patterns and principles they create and lay down for you and work endlessly to satisfy and meet the standards they have outlined and set for you—with minimal success and fulfillment on your part as the motives driving your actions are not from within you but from an external source.

It will be useful to look at some practical examples to enable us to better grasp this principle. Take, for instance, the reason why you eat is because you are hungry and the reason why you drink is because you are thirsty. Consequently, you will keep eating and/or drinking until you become satisfied and filled up. On the other hand, if you are not hungry or thirsty, there will be no intrinsic drive and, hence, motivation to eat or drink respectively. In the case of the former scenario (where you are now satisfied), irrespective of whether you are served your most favourite meal in the entire universe, you will have no drive to eat because you are full/satisfied and not hungry! Any attempt on your part to eat this favourite meal of yours in this condition will be greed/gluttony and will never produce a similar sense of satisfaction and fulfillment that would generally be derived if consumed when you were hungry and on an empty stomach.

In the same manner your thirst for water or hunger for food drives you to endlessly search for water or food respectively, without ceasing, until you eventually get hold of water or food to quench your desires; so too must your hunger and thirst for success be in order for you to be continually driven and motivated to pursue and achieve it at all cost! So, if you want to succeed in accomplishing your goals and experiencing great inner satisfaction and fulfilment, then your desire to succeed must be very strong and compelling enough to produce the exact same or similar sensation you would experience when you are very hungry and/or thirsty—an unstoppable drive that can only be extinguished via the satisfaction derived from eating and/or drinking! Any other drive for success falling short of such compulsion might not be strong enough to stand the test of time and hence may lead to reduced motivation/drive or lack of motivation to pursue success and, in certain instances, demotivation—as your motive is not compelling enough to drive and maintain success.

Therefore, as you make plans to step forth and fulfill your desired goals in the various areas of your life you must clearly identify and establish the motives behind every single goal you have identified and established and every plan and action you intend to take. Furthermore, you must also assess and evaluate whether your motives are well-founded and compelling enough to drive, accomplish, and maintain success. In this way, you are sure to stay on track and not go astray, be misled, stop, give up or quit—you are therefore sure to remain motivated and zealous throughout the journey until your ultimate goal is achieved and your hunger and thirst are satisfied and quenched.

In some cases, you may need to change your strategies and/or direction/course, yet your destination and motive for choosing that specific destination is assured and steadfast. Thus, you become less fearful and more courageous and confident about the choices and decisions you make on the way to accomplishing your goal/s because you have a clear knowledge and understanding of where you are heading to and a very compelling and distinctive why.

Now, before we proceed any further, I would like you to take some time and ask yourself repeatedly why you want to resolve those problems you have identified and achieve the desired results you have set out. You must ask these questions several times until your answers to them become certain and definite without ambiguity at any one moment in time. Your responses to these questions will henceforth determine how successful and resilient you become in the process of accomplishing your established goals.

A Guide to Establishing Your Motivation and Drive for Success

What is motivating and driving you to set and accomplish these goals? What are your reasons for embarking on this new journey? What are the reasons behind every goal set and every action to be taken?

Is your reason for embarking on this journey and accomplishing these goals to prove something to someone? Or is it to prove that other people were wrong about you or even to prove something to yourself? You have to make sure that you have the right motives and be very certain and unwavering about why you are doing this in the first place.

Here is a simple guideline to enable you to identify and establish whether your motives are right and will stand the test of time:

Evaluate and establish whether the motives behind your action will bring you immense satisfaction and fulfilment or resolve a problem. For example, if your response to any of the above questions is because you desire to solve an existing problem and bring about a lasting solution—then go for it. However, if it is to prove something or please someone else, then this is not a good enough motive, neither is it a "wrong motive"; nonetheless, it is not compelling enough. Therefore, if you are doing it for such reasons, then I am certain that it is not going to be lasting or sustainable ... nor will you be able to stand the test of time and persevere in times of great uncertainty/turbulence. This is so because the moment you become aware of the fact that the "said person" is not pleased anymore or that, regardless of how much effort you put in, you are not successful in satisfying that person's desires and standards, you will eventually become demotivated and give up. Consequently, you are no longer driven or motivated to carry on and keep going—for there is/are no obvious reason/s to do so anymore.

Unhealthy Motivation to Avoid When Setting Your Goals

Let me use the example of developing a healthier lifestyle and maintaining a definite weight to elaborate on this point and what I mean by the above statement. If I ask you, "Why do you want to weigh 70 kg and not 100 kg anymore or go down to 65 kg?" and, "Why do you want to walk 15 minutes every day throughout this year?" What will be your responses to the above questions? Your motives need to be very clear and definite. Will it be because all of your friends or colleagues are doing so or is it because summer is around the corner and almost everyone is working out just to fit into their summer costumes so they can go to the beach, and you want to do the same? Or is it because your spouse is not pleased with your current weight/lifestyle and keeps reminding you every day that you need to lose some weight? Is it because everyone around you makes fun of you and you want to prove to them that you can also be slim and healthy? Are you doing it because you've lost your self-esteem/confidence and feel depressed and ashamed in the midst of family and friends? And the list goes on...

If any of the above is your motive for setting and wanting to accomplish this goal, I would highly recommend that you stop now. Take some time out to re-evaluate and re-establish your motives. None of the above responses is a good enough reason—and therefore compelling enough to motivate you and keep you motivated until your goals are achieved. Besides, there is no personal fulfilment and satisfaction derived from the accomplishment and achievement of such goals set on the basis of the above foundation/motivation as your motive for setting and accomplishing them in the first place has got nothing to do with an intrinsic drive, personal satisfaction, and fulfillment! On the contrary, it has to do with pleasing/satisfying others, unhealthy competition, fear, and shame.

In addition, no matter how successful you are in accomplishing these goals and eventually arriving at your established weight of 70 kg, if your spouse, colleagues, and/or friends, still remain unsatisfied by your efforts and think that your achievements are not good enough or that 70 kg is still an unhealthy weight, then you will remain unsatisfied and unaccomplished as well—failing to recognise, acknowledge, and celebrate your efforts, milestones and success. What a tragedy!

Healthy and Commendable Motivation to Consider When Setting Your Goals

On the other hand, if your motive for embarking on this weight loss and healthy lifestyle journey is because:

1. You want to enjoy the beauty and benefits that come from being healthy—and consequently enjoy yourself and the marvellous creation that you are.

2. You are a loving mum or dad who wants to spend more quality time with her/his children, playing and running around with them without getting so exhausted and constantly running out of breath.

3. You want to spend more quality and valuable time with your spouse and family because you are fit, happier, and stronger...

Then I applaud you and encourage you to go for it; you couldn't be more right and motivated to achieve your goals and enjoy success! Based on such motives, you are definitely bound to kick-start, persist, and succeed in the process and eventually experience a deep sense of inner peace, satisfaction, and fulfilment in accomplishing your goals.

Of note, once your motives are about creating solutions, creating inner peace, rest, fulfilment, and a sense of satisfaction and worth, the results achieved go beyond benefiting a single individual and automatically overflow and benefit all those around you. For example, in this particular case, you actually become healthier and more active; you feel better, sleep better, and have more energy to run around and play with your children/grandchildren and spend more quality time with your spouse and/or children.

You don't get tired easily; you are more energetic and productive, qualities and traits that help to boost your creativity and performance and fuel you with the energy and mental strength to accomplish a lot of things, which will obviously benefit your children, spouse/partner and community as well.

Consequently, it should be about you and how you will feel after accomplishing your goal! Once you establish the motive for why you're doing what you are doing, or even thinking of doing it, then you are sure to be motivated to kick-start the project sooner than later and also stay the course, even at times when you don't feel like it or everything seems to be against you...

In order to successfully achieve your ideal weight of 70 kg and maintain an active lifestyle, it is vital that you are motivated to initiate the journey towards achieving your ideal and established weight and lifestyle; stay motivated and persistent; keep going/pressing on; and stay on the right path, maintaining the right habits that will lead to the achievement of your ideal weight—without derailing, going off track, or quitting. Finally, you should be able to achieve your ideal weight of 70 kg and maintain this weight and lifestyle without falling back into your old habits.

Also, be reminded that your journey towards achieving a healthier lifestyle and definite weight is a process and not an end result. It embodies the process/processes that will:

1. Enable you to initiate the steps that will lead to a healthier lifestyle;

2. Guide and help you to be disciplined and make the right choices that are required in order to achieve a healthier lifestyle and live in a healthy way and;

3. Equip and enable you to maintain a healthy weight and lifestyle.

I know of so many people who have set for themselves amazing and realistic health goals but unfortunately are unable to achieve these goals. They are motivated by peers and friends to start the process; then, after a few days or weeks, they stop and give up—they eat healthy one day or for a weekand the next day or week they eat unhealthily. Others even go as far as achieving their ideal weight and then put on more weight after a while and are back to where they started, or sometimes even worse.

Thus, it is all about the initiation, guidance, and maintenance process. Furthermore, when you lose sight of the driving force behind your goals or actions, sooner or later you are likely to give up—especially in the face of challenges. On the other hand, when you have the motivation and reason to carry on when those challenges come your way, you'll be motivated and inspired to keep going—because you know the satisfaction you will gain from achieving and fulfilling your goal/s.

> "Wanting something is not enough. You must hunger for it. Your motivation must be absolutely compelling in order to overcome the obstacles that will invariably come your way."
>
> **- Les Brown**

Healthy and Compelling Motivation is Fundamental and Indispensable for Your Success and Fulfilment

Before I got married and became a mother of three amazing children, my dress size was a size 10, and occasionally size eight, while my ideal weight was 55 kg, though I sometimes dropped to 50 kg when I worked out a lot more than usual. Generally speaking, I love and enjoy staying fit and looking good—in fact, it has become a lifestyle and an integral part of me. To me, it is all about experiencing optimal health and well-being and true transformation and beauty that flourishes from within. It is very obvious that whenever you are fit, healthy, and happy within, you are radiant and eventually flourish emotionally, mentally, and physically.

Consequently, when you flourish in optimal health and wellness, this state of being and experience automatically impacts and benefits your overall health and well-being, and everything/everyone around you, including your work, family, and relationships. You do not only feel

SUCCESS BLUEPRINT

contented but absolutely great and excited about life. To me, this is the true essence of life...

Hence, after each pregnancy and childbirth I am always keen and zealous to get back to my ideal dress size and weight, which are size 10 and 55 kg respectively. But as you will know from experience, particularly those of you who are also in the same boat and are trying so hard to shed some extra pounds (especially those gained during pregnancy and after childbirth) and attain a healthy weight and lifestyle, this is not a task for the fainthearted, undisciplined, and uncommitted/lazy. It takes courage, discipline, commitment, consistency, and hard work to lose a significant amount of weight and maintain a healthy weight and lifestyle—especially after pregnancy and childbirth.

Here I am, with every pregnancy and childbirth, comfortably becoming a size 14 and weighing up to 72 kg following the birth of my first two children and reaching an all-time high record of 80 kg, two months after the birth of my third child and last daughter! Despite all the challenges and discomfort that come with pregnancy and childbirth weight gain, I am always determined and committed to return to my ideal weight—usually by month nine following childbirth, giving myself enough time to enjoy motherhood and simply chill.

My profound and insatiable desire to become fit and healthy again, and ultimately return to my ideal dress size of 10 and weight of 55 kg, is always so powerful and compelling that I am reminded of this desire each day I wake up and step out of bed and every time I dress up, especially when I have to step out of the house, and I am compelled to spend hours looking for that ideal dress to wear! In fact, each time after childbirth, I have a complete wardrobe makeover, but I am always determined not to buy too much, lest I get comfortable and complacent with my new dress size!

Despite the weight challenges, these are some of the most precious, happiest, and fulfilled moments of my life—becoming a mother. I definitely do not get depressed or sad because of the excessive weight I tend to put on; rather, I concentrate on enjoying every single moment with my wonderful and gracious children while keeping a very positive outlook towards my ideal weight/lifestyle and health goals ... and celebrating the sacrifices my entire being goes through to bring them into this world.

My all-time strategy is first and foremost to accept and love the new me, yet never taking my eyes off my goal of getting back to the ideal me, which is far fitter, healthier, and more dynamic. I am also resolved and committed to enjoying and celebrating every stage of my health and weight-loss journey, irrespective of what my husband and/or loved ones think, say, or do!

On the other hand, my wonderful husband is always so obsessed about me returning to my premarital/pre-pregnancy weight and dress size, such that he will often get me a gift (usually a size-10 dress that I really love) just before I am due to give birth! To him, this is to inspire me and signify his expectation that I will return to my ideal weight after childbirth and fit into the dress! Nevertheless, my profound desire and zeal to return to my ideal weight and dress size has always been the key determining factor that drives and guarantees my success ...and it has never been about my husband's expectations or desires.

As much as I love him, it is always first and foremost about my health and my quest and hunger for a fit, fun, and healthy lifestyle again—which will eventually be of benefit not only to me but to him and our children/loved ones as well. Hence, I seize this unique opportunity to address, encourage, and inspire every woman or man out there reading this book right now and going through a similar challenge at the moment, especially if you are married and have children.

I deliberately made the choice to share my story here with you so as to inspire you to always be hopeful and never give up your desire for a healthy weight and lifestyle ... for if I could achieve this – not once, not twice, but thrice – then the chances are you too can do so, and most probably much quicker than I did because I am here to support you and provide you with a blueprint and a step-by-step guide, which, when applied consistently in any area of your life, will produce desired results and guaranteed success.

In addition, I am also sharing with you my greatest weight-loss strategy and success secret, which worked three times in a row and is still working now as I share this story with you and is profoundly embedded in my

WHY. Your WHY is and will forever remain the bedrock of your weight-loss journey and success ... so settle it in your mind once and for all before kick-starting your incredible journey.

I am very privileged to work with a huge number of women of all backgrounds, nationalities, races, cultures, status, and faiths and during the course of my work with them, either through workshops, mentoring, coaching, consultation, seminars, or conferences, one thing frequently stands out—irrespective of their background, nationality, race, culture, status, and/ or faith their tendency is to naturally conform and please others above themselves, especially their spouses/ partners and children. Amongst those dealing with the challenge of excessive weight gain (the majority of which is as a result of pregnancy and childbirth), over 80% have very low self-esteem and confidence and are subject to continuous pressure from their spouse/partner to lose the excess weight. Such pressure makes it even more stressful and difficult for them to be loyal towards a healthy pathway and lifestyle...

Yet, those who eventually decide to do something about their weight and health—anything, do so in an attempt to conform and please their spouse/partner without any compelling intrinsic drive and motivation. They go on doing everything and anything in their power to lose some weight in order to get the approval and recognition of their lovely spouse/ partner, which is often not the case... Too often, the seemingly little effort and

SUCCESS BLUEPRINT

progress, which are equally important in the overall process and result, go unnoticed and unappreciated.

A month passes by, then two months pass by, three months, and more months pass by with nothing to show as appreciation or celebration for the progress and milestones achieved thus far—absolutely nothing! Unfortunately, more often than not, these women too fail to acknowledge and celebrate the milestones achieved, thinking they haven't done enough, and feel more frustrated and depressed! While to their spouses/partners the bigger picture is more important than the details, and that is where their focus is—getting back to the ideal weight, nothing less and nothing more!

If this is also the case for you, then you will notice that the little and steady progress you make often goes unrecognised and unappreciated, due to the tiny nature of the achievement, when compared to that which is expected and still to be accomplished. In essence, it could be compared to taking a litre of water out of a mighty sea or ocean—very insignificant indeed, especially from a spectator's viewpoint. At this point in time, you are struggling with little or no external support and encouragement, which makes you become demotivated, in spite of all your hard work and determination, because your primary source of motivation is not from within but is externally driven. Hence, a lack of external push will result in a standstill, and subsequently withdrawal.

Therefore, in order to be steadfast and continually motivated to achieve your healthy lifestyle/weight loss goal/s, it is very crucial and fundamental that you clarify and know exactly why this weight loss journey and ideal weight/lifestyle you have chosen is important and beneficial! Furthermore, it is paramount that you establish the fact that you are doing it primarily for yourself because you profoundly desire and yearn to undertake this journey and path. Eventually, others will benefit from your decision and actions, and not the other way round.

Sustainable and Long-Lasting Benefits of a Healthy & Compelling Motivation

Of note, when your goal is fulfilled, you are happier, have a healthier relationship with yourself and others, and consequently experience a sense of accomplishment. People around you, especially your spouse/loved ones, will certainly experience and benefit from the positive energy, joy, and aura that radiates from you and around you. Below are some of the other benefits you and your spouse/loved ones will reap as a result of you fulfilling your weight loss and health goals.

Dropping from 100 kg to 70 kg and maintaining this new and ideal weight signifies a significant change in your habits and, hence, lifestyle—to a much healthier one. You will now have to eat healthily, and in doing so, you will be helping your spouse/family too. This will mean buying and cooking more healthy food and encouraging them to eat healthy, especially if you are female/a mother.

Research has shown that women make the majority of the shopping and spending decisions in their homes. So you will be making those decisions and choices to spend on healthy food and as a substitute for unhealthy ones. For example, if you and your family used to consume a lot of sweets, fizzy drinks, and juice, you may now substitute these with fresh fruits, fresh fruit juice, healthy drinks, and water.

A significant reduction in your weight and physical size definitely furnishes you with a lot more energy than before. In this state of well-being, you can fully enjoy life with your spouse and children and be there for them physically, emotionally, and psychologically.

There is also going to be a significant improvement and benefit to your spouse as becoming more physically active, fit, and flexible also means improving your relationship and making it more fun and exciting! Thus, you will be fulfilling and satisfying your heart's desires and his as well.

Most probably when you were a young couple or just got married (if you are married), your spouse would lift you up and run around with you as a way of expressing his love for you but stopped doing this due to your significant weight gain and the risk associated with lifting you up. However, with your new weight and active lifestyle, you are capable of living these truly unique moments and experiences again, which also indirectly encourages and motivates him to stay fit and healthy—first for himself then to mutually benefit both of you...

Dr Sylvia Forchap Likambi

I hereby encourage you to keep your eyes focused on the lasting and life-changing benefits you will reap by engaging and staying loyal/steadfast to your weight-loss and healthy lifestyle cause without giving up due to the temporary and momentary discomfort and discouragement you encounter along the way.

You must deny yourself the temporary pleasures and satisfaction you will gain from indulging in poor and unhealthy diets and habits/lifestyle in anticipation of the lasting and endless benefits you will reap from self-discipline and indulgence in healthy habits/lifestyle.

CHAPTER THREE
AMBITION

> *"Ambition is internally and individually driven—and an ambitious goal coupled with an ambitious individual is a powerful fuel and catalyst for success."*

Once you have established a clear motive for setting your goals, the third blueprint or rule of thumb/principle to consider and implement is the law of ambition. This law states that, "Ambition is internally and individually driven—and an ambitious goal coupled with an ambitious individual is a powerful fuel and catalyst for success." Now, ask yourself this critical question before proceeding any further: "Is my goal a very ambitious one and am I ambitious enough to accomplish it?"

Ambition is defined as a strong desire to do or achieve something—a desire and determination to achieve success. It is about utilising your maximum potential, ability, and resources to achieve success—and when it's not possible to rely solely on your potential, ability, and resources, you must be willing and ready to maximise and leverage the resources of your network and people around you to enable you accomplish your goals and success. Ambitious goals are in alignment with the laws of nature.

A Guide to Establish How Ambitious You Are

In order to establish how ambitious you are, and thus your probability of succeeding, you must be able to respond to the following questions:

- Do you have a great desire, the determination and willpower to accomplish your goals and achieve success?

- Are you ready and willing to invest and maximize all your strength, resources, and network to achieve your targeted goals?

- Are you challenged and stretched by your goals?

- Are you ambitious enough and have that strong desire and mental strength to keep going and pressing on until your goals are accomplished in every area that you set for yourself?

If you don't have the full ability and/or potential to accomplish your goals, you have to be willing to maximize your resources and those around you—it could be your network, you've got to maximize that.

A Guide to Establish How Ambitious Your Goals Are

It is not sufficient for you to be ambitious, you also need to ensure that your goal is ambitious enough to ignite a burning desire and determination within you to achieve it and succeed at all cost. If this is not the case, and you have a very lukewarm attitude towards your goal, then it is not an ambitious goal but merely another ordinary day-to-day activity/target or ritual and accomplishing it will not make any significant difference or impact in your life, neither will it result in a deep sense of satisfaction or fulfilment. Rather, it will just be another opportunity to tick your to-do list and evidence that you have been busy and not idle. However, you could be busy all day or all year long without ever being accomplished or fulfilled and still feel a void within.

Consequently, when referring to identifying, setting and accomplishing goals that lead to fulfilment and success, you should be more ambitious and avoid ordinary non-ambitious goals that neither stretch you nor make you grow and triumph.

Dr Sylvia Forchap Likambi

A Guide to Enable You to Identify and Avoid Unambitious Goals

Let's consider a typical example of an ordinary day-to-day activity, which must be distinguished from an ambitious goal. For example, you plan to drop your child off at nursery every morning at 8:00 a.m. before going to work and you plan to do that every single weekday throughout the new year... This is simply a daily routine/activity that is part of your day and every drop-off or pickup produces no real tangible satisfaction and fulfilment because this is just another activity ticked off your to-do list for the day. However, an ideal and more ambitious goal in a case like this would be:

- To get your child to get away from the comfort of your home and interacting with other children.

- To get your child to interact with other children and gain new social and communication skills.

- To get your child to learn and grow with other children and improve his/her confidence.

Such is ambitious with clear motives outlined and certainly will ignite a strong desire and determination within you to start searching for a nursery that will meet and fulfil your ultimate heart's desire and will for your child. You will wake up energised and determined every single day to achieve and accomplish this goal ... and once your ideal nursery for your child is secured, you will certainly be full of a deep sense of satisfaction and accomplishment. Nonetheless, it doesn't stop here. Each day, as you drop her off, you are excited to watch her interact with her little friends and the nursery staff. And when you pick her up, you are also excited to find out about her development and growth within the environment—with each new development bringing you immense satisfaction and fulfilment.

Do you notice a significant difference between identifying/setting an ambitious goal and simply setting ordinary day-to-day activities you want to achieve? Also, take note of how the motivation for doing this makes all the difference.

In order words, you must set highly challenging and ambitious goals that stretch and develop you daily—by constantly taking you out of your comfort zone and increasing your confidence. Now, re-examine your long list of goals and head for the ambitious ones to kick off your journey with great enthusiasm and for maximum performance and fulfilment. Addressing and accomplishing ambitious goals helps build your "ambitious muscles" and make you more ambitious and productive over time—building more positive energy and resilience within you.

> "It is a grand thing to rise in the world. The ambition to do so is the very salt of the earth. It is the parent of all enterprise, and the cause of all improvement."
>
> **- Anthony Trollope**

> "When you want to succeed as bad as you want to breathe, then you'll be successful."
>
> **- Eric Thomas**

CHAPTER FOUR

REALISATION

> *"Every thought conceived in the human mind becomes reality once written down and confessed—there are therefore no unrealistic goals, only unrealistic timing."*

Once you are certain that your goal is ambitious enough and you are equally ambitious and willing to make it a reality, you should move on to apply the fourth rule of thumb and law/principle—the law of realisation. Law brings your goals and visions into realisation and gives them the power to be made manifest as tangible ideals worthy of pursuit.

Realisation is defined as making real or giving the appearance of reality—it is an act of becoming fully aware of something as a fact.

Therefore, once you have identified and established an ambitious goal and are highly motivated and ambitious to accomplish it more than half the job is already done and you are now presented with a tangible reality waiting for you to drive it forward. Consequently, do not be preoccupied with thoughts of having realistic or unrealistic goals or what you lack or need in order to make it a reality. Too many people spend so much time carrying out unnecessary surveys and studies to identify whether or not their goals are realistic, practical, and/or attainable—in my opinion, this is a complete waste of time and resources. If you desire it badly enough, you will surely achieve it, as long as it is not for selfish reasons or destructive.

I have also heard managers, leaders, trainers, friends, and colleagues too often give advice to caution people about setting unrealistic goals and targets ... in actuality, they should be more concerned about unrealistic timings not goals because there's no unrealistic goal or vision; every goal or vision is an idea/thought conceived in the mind and whatever the human mind thinks and conceives has the potential of becoming reality and physically experienced.

The one independent factor that largely determines and drives the realisation of your goal is desire... How much do you desire to accomplish your goals, solve a problem, and achieve success? Consequently, you need to start embracing and visualising your goals and vision as your ideals—something that you profoundly desire and hope for and which is obtainable. It is something that is within your mind and you are capable of creating it in reality once you write it down as a goal. The only setback, or reason why its physical manifestation could be delayed, is the timing.

Of note, your vision is an internalised mental image of your ideal life or a preferable future, a mental picture of your purpose of existence; it is seeing much further and deeper than your physical eyes or anyone around you could ever be able to see—and whatever you can see you can achieve. Once you have seen a clear picture of what you desire in your mind, for as long as it is in your mind it is only an idea/a thought in your mind. Therefore, you need to be able to project the idea/thought onto a blank screen or blank sheet of paper by writing it down, confessing it, and giving it life. Remember, the power of death and life lies in the tongue. Once written and expressed as your ideal life, it automatically becomes a reality at that point. When I talk of reality, I'm talking about being practical or attainable over a given and appropriate timescale. Hence, it is not immediately tangible at conception—it is a conceived idea/thought within your mind and only becomes reality through your deliberate creation and allowing. Therefore, it is your sole responsibility and decision to envisage your vision; set the goals required to achieve it; write them down; confess them; create them; and make them a tangible reality.

Dr Sylvia Forchap Likambi

A Step-by-Step Guide to Enable You Bring Your Goal into Realisation

Let's assume that one of your goals is to become an ambitious and successful lawyer. This is a very realistic goal, irrespective of your background, economic and social status, nationality, age, gender, and current life circumstances. Nonetheless, a two-year-old child would not expect to become a lawyer at the age of two, four, or even six. Neither would a grown-up and well-educated adult expect to become a lawyer overnight—this would be unrealistic as the goal could not be attained in a day or even in a week or month! There is a process, and this requires time. Therefore, to be reasonable and realistic, you need to give yourself enough time in order to successfully become a lawyer. Goal setting and accomplishment is definitely an elaborate and fine-tuned process that requires a step-by-step procedure and sufficient time. In a case like this, you will need to break it down into sizeable chunks and little steps to be immediately implemented and accomplished.

Another good example is setting a goal to become a doctor overnight—you would never be able to become a doctor overnight, just as with becoming a lawyer. There is a process involved—intense training is needed. Be reasonable and give yourself some time and clearly map out/record the little steps/strides and milestones to be taken and completed as they represent evidence of realisation. As with the case of the lawyer, you will also need to break down your goal/s into little chunks to be accomplished over a reasonable time while recognising, acknowledging, and celebrating every single step you take to move closer to achieving your goals/vision and making them a tangible reality. Be reasonable and practical when setting your goals in terms of the timing you allocate to achieving the main goal and each milestone.

You must be aware of the fact that any goal that has already been accomplished by any human on planet Earth is realistic and achievable, while any goal you set that has not yet been accomplished by anyone definitely makes you the first person to ever set and accomplish such goal—which is also achievable. You are definitely the pioneer in this area. If you ever conceived the thought within your mind, then go for it because it is achievable and realistic.

For example, if your goal is to gain a healthier lifestyle and weight in the new year and the years ahead, how will this come into realisation? How long will you require to accomplish and make this goal a reality and true success? Now, it doesn't matter how big you are—neither does your background, economic and/or social status matter. However, you should be able to live and experience this lifestyle in reality, not only in your mind—in this way you are more motivated and excited to accomplish it.

In the process of realising your big dream/goal, you could start by implementing practical little steps like this: waking up earlier to exercise; eating more fruits and vegetables; drinking loads of water, etc. Such little steps and milestones could be easily recorded and accounted for. In fact, you can literally tell what you ate for breakfast, if you have been to the gym or not, and whether or not you have drunk plenty of water.

Imagine you were a size 16; it wouldn't be reasonable or practical for you to think that you could get into a size eight in one day or even in one week! So please be reasonable so you don't get discouraged and give up along the way—remember to stay on the path and not to slip off when you face those challenges.

Now, write down 10 mini goals or baby steps you will take in order to fulfil your first and most important goal... In other words, write down a list of things you will do or steps to take to arrive at your final destination. Do the same for every major and significant goal you have identified and set in other areas of your life/personal development. In this way, your goals will become more tangible and a practical reality.

SUCCESS BLUEPRINT

> *"The positive thinker sees the invisible, feels the intangible and achieves the impossible."*
> **- Winston Churchill**

> *"Anything is possible. Dream! Reach out! Achieve!"*
> **- Lailah Gifty Akita**

> *"I can do all things through Christ, who strengthens me."*
> **- Philippians 4:13**

> *"There is no limit to what you can achieve if you put in great effort towards the fulfillment of your dreams."*
> **- Lailah Gifty Akita**

CHAPTER FIVE

TIME

> *"Time is definitive and waits for no one—you are either flowing with time or it is flowing past you."*

The fifth blueprint or rule of thumb to consider and implement is the law of time. This law states that, "Time is definitive and waits for no one - you are either flowing with time or it is flowing past you." Do not put off the things you must do today and now until tomorrow or another time. What you must do now do now, and what you must do tomorrow do tomorrow.

Avoid procrastination today and always, and get into the habit of taking action when it is needed. This is paramount if you desire to be successful and fulfill your purpose in life. We all have 24 hours in a day. Have you ever wondered why some people are so successful and fulfilled and others not? You must effectively utilize the time you have been blessed with while here on Earth ... for every second gone, we will never be able to get it back, so too are the amazing opportunities gone with it! Arise and take action while you still have the time to do so.

In order to achieve complete realisation of your goal/s and give it/them a tangible presence and expression, you must consider and implement the fifth blueprint and rule of thumb/principle—the law of time. At this stage of your journey to accomplishing your goals, you will need to set a time frame and be time-bound. You need to put a time limit beside every goal of yours, commencing with your top priority. Let's say that you're really great at working within constraints. With great motivation, you're pushed to work within the constraints of a time frame. It will greatly help you if you implement this rule of thumb/law in your life. You are required to put a deadline on all of your goals and sub goals and keep in mind that you need to act before these deadlines—which requires discipline.

Let's consider a simple practical example to understand how important and motivating it could be when we put a deadline on our tasks/goals. Have you realised that most parents put off buying children's school uniforms when they are on holidays and have ample time for shopping? On the contrary, you will notice that just few days before the children resume school after a long holiday, many parents and families queue up in the shops to buy their children's school uniforms, causing so much congestion and delay. Every parent seems to be looking at buying their children's uniforms during this time. Why is this so? There is a time frame in question; the holidays are now over and schools will be resuming—hence the children need to go to school with their uniforms. At this point in time, whether you feel like going to the shops or not, there is very little you can do now. Time will not and does not wait for anyone. Therefore, if you do not catch up with it and act within the required timescale, you will be left behind, and there will be consequences for such actions. Hence, the time frame makes you realize that you need to get your child's school uniforms now before schools resume.

Let me give you another example that highlights the significance of introducing a time frame when setting your goals. Imagine your child is unwell and has been prescribed some medications that you need to collect from the pharmacy. Let's assume you have been out working all day and are really tired and would love to go home and rest ... nonetheless, you are told that the pharmacy closes in an hour and your daughter needs to start her medication that evening. You will definitely go and get the medication for your daughter, irrespective of how tired you feel, because you are aware of the fact that you have got very limited time to do so before the pharmacy closes.

Do you remember during those school days when a day before your exams you were capable of cramming an entire chapter of a book or even an entire book? Do you also remember that, very close to the examination day or on the vigil of the exams, you were capable of staying up all night long to read and prepare for the exams and even using some hash and drastic measures to keep you awake during the night? Do you also remember that during the final hours prior to the exams, you became more alert and capable of understanding concepts that you were not able to understand/comprehend all year long? What suddenly happened to you a night prior to the exams? Why did you suddenly become more alert? Why did you seem to understand faster than before? Why were you able to cram an entire chapter or book you weren't able to cram during the academic year? Timing! The examination day is fast approaching and everything, including nature, works in your favour...

Usually, when you have a deadline, you get stressed and your body produces stress hormones such as cortisol and adrenaline that fuel your energy and cause you to take action; this often happens close to important deadlines, life events, and examinations. Generally speaking, stress is good for you as it helps to remind you/your system that you need to take action for a definite purpose. When your "adrenaline is pumping", you're more alert and driven to act within a given time frame.

In order to provide you with the much needed strength and energy (that you did not originally possess in your dormant/undisturbed and laid back state) or to enable you to fully exploit the potential stored/unused energy within you, more adrenaline, cortisol, dopamine, and other stress-related hormones are being released. These hormones enable your heartbeat to increase, your muscles to contract faster, etc. so as to enable you to engage in the "Fight or Flight" process of a physiological battle. At this stage, you are well equipped and capable of taking actions you would not have taken and quicker than usual too.

Once the action has been taken, these chemicals/stress hormones are then reabsorbed/broken down because your brain is aware of the fact that the threat is being dealt with or taken off, and therefore there is no longer any reason or need to amplify the signal and thus provide feedback—which then enables you to relax and rest.

A typical example of how to time bind your goals is to say, for example, from January to March, I must weigh 85 kg—that is moving from 100 kg to 85 kg and losing a total of 15 kgs, which is measurable. A more effective way to do this, which will help you develop your time management skills, is to have a journal in which you record your yearly, monthly, weekly, and daily goals—of note, these should be goals and not activities. In this way you become more time conscious and focused on your goals and on carrying out those activities required to accomplish them. For example, with respect to your health and fitness goal, you could write down all that you would like to accomplish in this area by the end of the year, by the end of each month, by the end of each new week, and by the end of each new day – prior to the start of the year, month, week, and day – and follow through. Below is a template to assist you do this:

1) Yearly Goals: Write down all that you would like to achieve by the end of the year.

_____
_____
_____
_____

Monthly Goals: Write down all that you would like to achieve by the end of every new month.

_____
_____
_____
_____

Weekly Goals: Write down all that you would like to achieve by end of every new week.

_____
_____
_____
_____

Daily Goals: Write down all that you would like to achieve by end of every new day.

SUCCESS BLUEPRINT

_____
_____
_____
_____
_____

> "Yesterday is gone. Tomorrow has not yet come. We have only today. Let us begin."
> **- Mother Teresa**

> "Time is the longest distance between your dreams and reality."
> **- Dr Sylvia Forchap-Likambi**

CHAPTER SIX

ACTION

> *"Until accompanied by an action, your goals are mere wishes and dreams."*

The sixth blueprint or rule of thumb is the rule of action. This law states that, "Until accompanied by an action, your goals are mere wishes and dreams." Once you have identified and set your yearly, monthly, weekly, and daily goals to be accomplished within the specific time frames, if no action is taken, all such goals and visions become meaningless and could be compared to a beautifully framed picture hanging on the wall in your living room for decoration—regardless of how beautiful or detailed the picture is, it is static and will remain a picture forever. Therefore, for the realisation of your goals/vision to be possible so you can become successful and fulfilled, they must be accompanied by practical steps and actions, regardless of how small such may be. You must take action. Note that action is a doing thing—it is not a thinking or talking thing; therefore, just do it! Act now! Not later, not tomorrow, not in a week's time, but now! Let today's goals be accomplished today and now.

> *"Every action geared towards accomplishing your vision and goals is worthy and deserves recognition and acknowledgement."*

Never underestimate the significance of a single step on a journey of a thousand miles. Each step or action is fuel for the next—do whatever it is that will take you a step closer to your goals... After setting all of these amazing and time-bound goals for your life, if you just sit there, looking at them each day – visualising, affirming, praying, and confessing them day and night and multiple times during the day – without ever taking the necessary actions required to accomplish them, no amount of the Law of Attraction, Positivity, Faith, and/or Prayer will bring your goals to realisation. There is certainly a place and a time for praying, optimism, visualization, faith, etc., however, they cannot and should never be substitutes for action. Faith without works is dead. It is as simple as that. The Lord will order your steps, not move them; you need to

SUCCESS BLUEPRINT

make the move. Regardless of how small that move may be, just move! Every action geared towards the accomplishment of your goal is worthy, and deserves recognition and acknowledgement, and acts as fuel to motivate you and move you to the next stage of your journey.

One of the things that often hold people back and prevent them from acting is their continuous search for that which they need or lack in order to act. When your focus is on the things or resources that you do not have or would need in order to take action, it is very difficult to act—hence, frustration and anxiety step in and you appear helpless and unable to take full control or even partial control of the situation at hand. All of the above lead to fear—you become fearful; you withdraw and eventually freeze up! I encourage you to act with what you already have in your possession without giving it a second thought—you must channel all your energy and focus into what you have at hand, your greatest strengths and resources. In other words, ask yourself this question: "What have I got in my hands?" Too often in life, we look away from us—in search of that which we already possess.

Now, before you start thinking, *I may need new skills to be able to resolve and overcome this problem,* my question to you is this: what skills do you already possess? What strengths do you already have? Focus on your strengths, exploit and maximize them to the fullest. Consequently, all that you really need to do is just start. Do not worry about how or what you will need in order to achieve your goal. Once you kick-start the process, every other thing will eventually fall into place—and the law of inertia, which states that an object either remains at rest or continues to move at a constant velocity unless acted upon by a force, will kick in and work in your favour.

Action increases your confidence over time and makes you less prone to anxiety and depression—it fuels you with more energy and strength to keep going and stay on track until your goal is achieved. You may feel stressed initially, but this is good news as stress is a physiological condition that occurs when your body responds to external/internal stimulants or threats to protect and preserve you. If no action is taken, the messages/messengers/chemical release are amplified—a situation that leads to chronic stress and, if it persists, eventually leads to anxiety (as you tend to worry and feel helpless, unable to manage and/or control the situation) and depression (as a result of the chemical imbalances within your system and body). Such chemical imbalances eventually affect your other organs too, resulting in further complications and making you more unwell.

> "Action expresses priorities."
>
> **- Mahatma Gandhi**

Now, while taking a step at a time, you should acknowledge every bit of progress made and celebrate those seemingly little steps of progress and milestones achieved thus far. Each action or step taken fuels you with energy and provides you with more strength, tenacity, and

SUCCESS BLUEPRINT

motivation and drive to carry on. The bigger the action, the greater the fuel and drive to carry on and keep pressing on until your goal is achieved.

I recommend that, when you set out to act, you always start with the most significant action that will produce maximum yield and results and consequently a greater motivation to achieve. You should consider implementing the 80/20 Rule, also known as the Pareto Principle. This principle states that there is an imbalance between causes and results, between effort and reward, and the majority of what we do each day has little impact or benefits in our lives, while a small minority of our daily activities has the greatest and most significant impact. In simple and practical terms, this principle states that 80% of the activities in your to-do list collectively produce only 20% of your results, while the remaining 20% produce up to 80% of your results. Therefore, you must seek to identify and establish your 20% maximum yield activities, prior to commencing action, so as to avoid unnecessary waste of time and effort.

A useful tool or guide to enable you identify and set your priorities is the ABCDE Time Management method by Brian Tracy. This principle works on the basis that, although you may barely have enough time to accomplish every action on your to-do list, there is always enough time to do the most important things. Hence, you must focus on them until they are completed.

Let's examine in more detail how this method works and what the letters A, B, C, D, and E signify. You are required and encouraged to write down one of these letters in the margin before each of the tasks on your list, according to importance, prior to taking action.

"A" stands for "very important." This is an activity you must do, which has profound benefits and rewards if completed and huge negative consequences if not accomplished.

"B" stands for "important": an activity you should do, but it is not as important as "A" tasks and has minor negative consequences if not completed.

"C" stands for activities that are "nice to do" but they are not as important as "A" or "B" tasks, and there are no negative consequences for not completing them.

"D" stands for "delegate." This is an activity you can assign to someone else, who can do the task on your behalf.

"E" stands for "eliminate" and refers to activities you should eliminate whenever possible.

When you use the A-B-C-D-E method, you can very easily sort out what is important and unimportant to you and hence eliminate all unimportant time-consuming activities that only yield about 20% of your results.

> "The Distance Between Your Dreams and Reality is called ACTION."

> "There are only two rules for being successful. One, figure out exactly what you want to do, and two, do it."
>
> **- Mario Cuomo**

CHAPTER SEVEN

REST

> *"After all is done, it's time to sit back and relax in confidence and watch the principle of sowing and reaping work on your behalf."*

The seventh and the final blueprint or rule of thumb to implement is the law of rest. It states that, "After all is done, it's time to sit back and relax in confidence and watch the principle of sowing and reaping work on your behalf."

Have you done everything from investing time to identifying who you truly are and what you want in life in order to be successful and established very clearly why you want that? Have you also set those very ambitious goals and targets you would love to achieve and are you equally ambitious and determined to employ all your strengths, maximum ability, resources, network, and available opportunities to succeed? Have you clearly mapped out a definite blueprint/route, milestones, and timescales and made up your mind to execute your plan with all that you have in your possession and beyond?

Finally, have you executed all that you planned to and are you eventually navigating towards the milestones and road marks that lead to your final destination and goal/s? Well done, and many congratulations ... you deserve a big pat on the back and acknowledgement for how far you have travelled and come. Now is the time to put on the autopilot, sit back, relax, and enjoy your amazing ride and journey while you diligently wait for the harvest—as the laws of nature work on your behalf.

Don't be so caught up in the "doing" and the act of accomplishing your goals and achieving success that you fail to appreciate and enjoy the journey and the beauty of nature—the amazing and refreshing atmosphere/people you meet along the way and each milestone accomplished. You have done your part; now is the time for all that is in nature – rain, sunshine, wind, including the storms – to push and propel you forward and further towards your destination, with minimal effort from you. It's finally the end of a season and the beginning of another—it's an end to the season of sowing and the beginning of the season of natural growth and maturation that automatically leads into the season of harvest.

SUCCESS BLUEPRINT

Nature is working on your behalf and for you—the law of sowing and reaping, the law of attraction, the law of giving and receiving, etc., are all working on your behalf. Whatever you sowed you will be sure to reap in due season, and much more because the law of nature that results in the multiplication of your seed is also working for you and in your favour. Whatever you desired and envisaged you will attract—as the law of attraction is also working in your favour. Relax, revive, and enjoy life while you wait for a bountiful and gracious harvest in due season.

Now take note, resting is not for those that have not ploughed the land or sowed as there will be nothing to wait for in anticipation of the harvest. There will be no harvest without sowing—if this is expected, it will be considered "an illusion" and, in the worst case, stealing. In addition, resting is not for those without expectations as there will be nothing for those without expectations. Your degree of desire and expectation determines how much you will sow and eventually reap. Finally, resting is for the one who has been active and productive and now needs time to rejuvenate, refresh, revive and restore his/her energy—ready to bounce back again with enthusiasm and passion.

God has modelled the way for us by showing us when to rest. During Creation, He worked hard and continuously for six days and six nights, without ceasing—celebrating each milestone and achievement accomplished, day after day. After all was created and completed, He stepped back, acknowledged and celebrated His creation, and rested on the seventh day with profound confidence in His work and creation, destined to yield the fruits that were intended. In fact, He rested after He had created the world ... or the foundation of the world upon which He would build and establish His people.

In the same manner, you qualify for a worthy rest after you have created something. Rest is not for the lazy but the ambitious, determined, and innovative. Resting when you have not created will yield no fruits. In fact, it may even subtract from you—that is get you into debt, because the law of sowing and reaping works for and on behalf of every one existing on the planet—always bringing your way an excess of that which you sowed. Therefore, sowing nothing leads to reaping an excess of nothing, which results in a negative. In effect, you owe nature ... it's been providing you credit to live and enjoy life and you have never utilised or maximised/invested in it or given back to it.

Just as when it rains it waters every plant under the heavens – whether planted by the good or the bad, rich or poor, literate or illiterate, male, or female, black or white – so too it is in the season of harvest. Everyone who has sown must reap and in abundance— irrespective of their past, present, life circumstances, status, or background. This is the moment of truth and justice. It is the moment when nature yields and returns to you all that you have offered to it and much more. These are powerful life principles, which, if understood and applied, make

SUCCESS BLUEPRINT

success inevitable. Success is not based on how good, rich, well educated, etc. you are—rather it is based on the continuous application of specific success blueprint/principles and laws in every area of your life.

Consequently, having sown what you desired in the amazing new and fertile soil provided to you and me during this season, be rest assured of your bountiful harvest during the season of harvest. You need not panic/be anxious, troubled or disappointed during the season of nourishment and growth; master and understand the seasons and take some time to rest during this season following the season of ploughing and sowing, knowing that there is a time and a season for everything under the sun. Furthermore, based on the type of seed you have sown, there will be different waiting times, longer for some seeds and shorter for others—thus requiring more patience in some cases while you wait. Most importantly, you will be provided with the fruits that derive from the exact seed type you have sown and not otherwise.

Dr Sylvia Forchap Likambi

This now takes us back to the very beginning of this book—when you were provided with fertile soil/a brand-new land and platform to sow that which you desired. Therefore, if you have sown tomatoes, for example, you must expect to reap tomatoes. If you sowed mangoes then your harvest will be mangoes, and so on. Consequently, success is predictable and very deliberate too; your year and future are predictable. After every moment of harvest you must enjoy and delight in the fruits of your labour before preparing for the next season to sow again.

> *"When you find yourself in the thickness of pursuing a goal or dream, stop only to rest. Momentum builds success."*
> **- Suzy Kassem**

> *"Don't judge each day by the harvest that you reap but by the seeds that you plant."*
> **- Robert Louis Stevenson**

CHAPTER EIGHT

A Guide to Enable You to Identify Key Areas in Your Life Where You Could Effectively Set Desired Goals

To round up, I will now provide you with a detailed guide to support and enable you identify and effectively set and accomplish your desired goals and achieve success in every area of your life. This guide will enable you to evaluate your life and review some of the things that you have not yet identified and that you will really want to achieve in life, or in areas where you have a very vague idea.

To avoid ambiguity and confusion while setting your goals, I would like to narrow it down for you and encourage you to look at the following seven areas of your life and let your focus be around these areas.

1) Spiritual Development: Ask yourself what results you want to see in this area of your life to be able to confidently and undoubtedly say that you are successful and fulfilled when it comes to your spiritual life. What solutions do you want to bring about in terms of your spiritual development? What makes you spiritually fulfilled? For example, it may be spending more time in prayer or in meditation each day, showing more love and compassion towards yourself and those around you, etc.

Now, write down the results you would like to achieve in this area of your life in order to attain profound spiritual growth and success.

_____
_____
_____
_____
_____
_____
_____
_____
_____
_____
_____
_____
_____

SUCCESS BLUEPRINT

_____
_____
_____
_____
_____

_____
_____
_____
_____

2) Personal Development: What results or changes do you want to create in this area of your life in order to successfully develop to your full potential? In terms of your personal growth and character, what do you want to resolve? What positive and lasting results results do you want to see in this area of your life? For example, you may want to have a more positive attitude by creating and cultivating habits that are positive. You may want to become very courageous and confident by developing a higher self-esteem and immense trust in yourself. Make sure that you write them down and be very specific. Once you're done with your personal development, look at the next area.

_____
_____
_____
_____

Dr Sylvia Forchap Likambi

SUCCESS BLUEPRINT

_____
_____
_____
_____
_____

3) Relationships: You may want to establish what a successful relationship means. You may have to start by identifying and defining what a successful relationship with yourself means and what type of relationship you would love to have with yourself and eventually others. What results do you want to see in the area of your relationships? What harvest do you want to yield in this area? Establish what types of changes you will need to make in your relationships with your children, family, etc. in order to experience successful and fulfilling relationships. If you already have thriving and successful relationships, then you may want to look at the types of things you can do to improve these relationships that will benefit you and your loved ones more. Write them down and make plans to start working on them immediately. Once you've identified these and written them down, let's move on to another crucial area of your life.

_____
_____
_____
_____
_____

Dr Sylvia Forchap Likambi

SUCCESS BLUEPRINT

_____
_____
_____
_____

_____
_____
_____
_____

_____
_____
_____

4) Health and Well-Being: What does health and wellbeing success mean to you? What results do you want to achieve in the area of your health and well-being that will enable you to attain optimal health and well-being? In order to live a fulfilled and successful life of purpose, it is paramount that your health is in optimal condition. When I talk about your overall health and well-being, I am not just talking about your physical health. It is not about having your ideal or perfect weight and/or dress size; It is much more profound—it is about being spiritually, mentally, physically, and emotionally healthy and sound.

In order to flourish in optimal health, you must thrive to achieve harmony when it comes to your spiritual, mental, physical, and emotional well-being. You you have to look at these areas of your life and figure out what you must do to achieve equilibrium and harmony. What do you want to solve or resolve? What solutions do you want to achieve in these areas of your life? What results do you want to achieve in the area of your health and well-being? Think about it because investing in and working on your health will enable you to become stronger, healthier, and more energetic and fit to go out and impact the world/fulfil your purpose of existence.

_____
_____
_____
_____
_____
_____
_____
_____
_____
_____
_____
_____
_____
_____
_____
_____
_____
_____

SUCCESS BLUEPRINT

_____
_____
_____
_____
_____
_____
_____
_____
_____
_____
_____
_____
_____
_____
_____
_____
_____
_____
_____
_____

5) Career: Ask yourself what career or business success means to you. What do you want to achieve in the area of your career in order to be successful and fulfilled? What would you love to do and who would you love to become in order to live a purposeful and fulfilled life and, hence, be successful? What results do you want to generate so as to fulfil your vision and ideal career in life? What other results do you want to witness in the area of your career that will create career success? Write them down.

6) Rest & Relaxation: In terms of rest, you can't work all the time without taking a break and getting some rest. For example, you can't work continuously for 24 hours in a day without resting and sleeping. It is vital to have balance and harmony in every area of your life so you may flourish in optimal health and well-being and enjoy true success and fulfillment/inner peace. Always remember that in order for you to step out there and help others/your children and successfully impact more lives it is vital that you are healthy, fit, and alive—and I cannot emphasize this enough. Therefore, you need to rest, revive, and refresh to regain/restore your energy and the strength to carry on and keep going, being conscious of the fact that success is not a destination; rather, it is a lifestyle ... it is about becoming all that we were born and destined to become. As long as you still have breath in you, there's is still so much success awaiting you...

Nonetheless, as with every other area, you need to be able to clearly figure out what resting means to you and apply that in your life. For example, it may simply mean getting more sleep, taking a vacation, creating more time for yourself, or getting some relaxation and holistic therapies/sessions, etc. You deserve it—your body, mind, soul, and spirit sure deserve this and will be nourished by such. Now, write down the solutions you want to experience in this area of your life as you journey through a truly glorious, fulfilling, and successful life.

_____
_____
_____
_____
_____

SUCCESS BLUEPRINT

Dr Sylvia Forchap Likambi

Wealth: Wealth could be defined as an abundance of valuable possessions or money. Valuable possessions could be your life, your health and well-being, your relationships, your family, and loved ones. You need to determine what wealth means to you, which is different from financial rewards or riches. You could be rich but not necessarily wealthy. Rich people are motivated by money, while wealthy people are motivated and driven by their dreams, passions, and purpose/success.

In essence, to be successful simply means to be wealthy. In other words, when you are successful, you are experiencing abundance in every area of your life and are contented and profoundly fulfilled—devoid of any lack/poverty mentality/mindset. Your mindset is that of abundance and you understand that sharing your wealth only enriches you and others more as you continue to pour from the overflow of your abundance and are constantly and continuously being replenished. Hence, being successful does not necessarily mean becoming financially and materially rich while devoid of that deep inner peace, satisfaction and fulfillment that accompanies true success and wealth.

Consequently, you need to ask yourself these questions: "What does being wealthy mean to me? What kind of wealth do I want to create? What kind of legacy do I want to leave for my children/the world?" Write them down.

Once you start living a life of purpose, you are bound to become wealthy and successful. It's often said that you

SUCCESS BLUEPRINT

would never be able to achieve wealth by working a nine-to-five job or as an employee driven by a wage. On the contrary, wealth is created when you start exploiting and maximising your natural gifts and full potential and working towards fulfilling your purpose. Now write down in the space below what you desire to create or achieve in this area of your life, which will literally defines your success.

_____
_____
_____
_____
_____
_____
_____
_____
_____
_____
_____
_____
_____
_____
_____
_____
_____
_____
_____

Dr Sylvia Forchap Likambi

CONCLUSION

We have now come to the end of your blueprint/road map to success, and I would like you to take some time and reflect as you read through the final pages of this manuscript. I would like you to ask yourself one more time why you want to be able to accomplish all the goals you have identified and written down in the various areas of your life and become successful. What is your ultimate motive for wanting to accomplish all of these goals and eventually succeed in doing so? Remember to write down your motives here again, even if you have already done so in the previous chapters. It is important that your motive/s is/are consistent and unchanging. If they differ and continuously change, you will need some more time to resolve this and become very convinced and confident with your responses. This is crucial as your motive/s is/ are your greatest fuel to drive you forward and keep you going, thereby guaranteeing your success amidst the endless challenges and storms you will encounter along the way.

Of note, I would like to remind you that writing down all ultimate/ideal goals and motives is simply not enough—you need the wisdom to be able to effectively execute them and bring them into tangible realisation. It is usually said that knowledge is power; however, it is wisdom (the application of knowledge) that is true power and that can ultimately bring about genuine transformation and success in life.

So my final question to you is this: after all you have read and acquired, what knowledge are you going to take away from all that you have read in this book and apply in the relevant areas of your life? Not everything may be relevant in your life or circumstances—yet, you need to be able to identify what is relevant to you and then take it with you and eventually apply it in your life, in the area of relevance. You need to make the decision to apply it in your life today – not tomorrow, and now, not later – so that you will be able to live a fulfilled and successful life now and in the future.

Consequently, the most important step of all – which will result in a successful life/lifestyle – is ACTION! Faith, passion, ambition, etc. without works are simply dead. I hereby encourage you to make sure that you can take the necessary actions needed to drive your goals to accomplishment. Now, write down the necessary actions you intend to take as you get ready to close and put away this book—if you haven't yet done so! Remember, this is a blueprint and manual, so you may need to refer to it quite often, whenever needed or if you get lost/go off-track as you navigate through your journey to success.

SUCCESS BLUEPRINT

It is okay to stop every now and again and reflect at every given moment and opportunity on all that which you've written down—on the solutions that you would love to create in your life, family and/or world and why you want to create them, how ambitious you are to attain them. Reflect and focus on your inner strength and desire to keep going until you succeed—utilising and maximising your full potential and available resources to enable you to succeed.

Now, give yourself a deadline when you expect each one of these goals to be accomplished and be highly optimistic about every deadline. Yet, be reasonable and flexible as you make this a reality, being very kind and gentle to yourself at all times. Above all, don't put yourself down when you do not achieve your goals within the dedicated time frame or even get them wrong! It's perfectly alright. Acknowledge where you are in your journey at the moment, where you have come from, how far you have come, and pat yourself on the back, and tell yourself that it is all okay and it will continue to be okay. Do away with any thought of failure, reminding yourself that your purpose is to succeed in all your endevours and in every area of your life and there are really no failures in life but merely feedback.

You never really fail until you finally give up and accept defeat. Get up; dust yourself off; trust yourself again and in your inherent abilty to succeed, and start all over again or from where you stopped or encountered a setback/obstacle. In all this, remember to stay positive/optimistic because your mind works best when flooded with positive emotions, thoughts, and instructions. Hence, you might want to visualize and put a mental picture of what you desire to achieve in your mind—so that you have the passion and the energy to go ahead and fulfil that vision.

To Your Success and Greatness!

Success is a reality awaiting your arrival... Start your jouney today, now!

SUCCESS BLUEPRINT

Reader's Blueprint

Dr Sylvia Forchap Likambi

Reader's Blueprint

Dr Sylvia Forchap Likambi

SUCCESS BLUEPRINT

Reader's Blueprint

Dr Sylvia Forchap Likambi

SUCCESS BLUEPRINT

Reader's Blueprint

Dr Sylvia Forchap Likambi

AUTHOR'S BIOGRAPHY

Dr Sylvia Forchap-Likambi is a visionary, multi-award-winning leading empowerment and transformation authority, transformational speaker/coach, and three-time international best-selling author, specialising in the delivery of very high-quality/cutting-edge empowerment and revolutionary leadership and transformation programs. She is the founder and CEO of "Behaviour Changed" award-winning community interest company, Voice of Nations, and founder/global chair of The Global Visionary Women Network and global CEO/consultant of Dr Sylvia Likambi International/Dr Sylvia Likambi International Health & Well-being Clinic.

Over the years, she has coached, empowered, inspired, and positively impacted/transformed over one and a half million lives globally, including thousands of female entrepreneurs, and relentlessly empowered many to come out of addictions and depression and get into training, volunteering, employment/self-employment, and even leadership roles and also offered them several such opportunities through her organisations.

She has featured on several national and international radio and TV stations and been guest/keynote speaker to several national and international audiences, ranging from community groups to universities. For more information about Dr Sylvia Forchap-Likambi and her work, or to invite her for an interview or to deliver some of her cutting-edge transformational programs and talks to your team or company, please contact her using the details below:

Email: forchaps@drsylvialikambi.com

Tel: +44 (0) 7539 216072

- www.voiceofnations.org.uk
- www.globalvisionarywomennetwork.org
- www.drsylvialikambi.com

Website:

www.likambiglobalpublishing.com

Email:

enquiries@likambiglobalpublishing.com

Address:

208a Picton Road, Liverpool, L15 4LL

United Kingdom

www.ingramcontent.com/pod-product-compliance
Lightning Source LLC
Chambersburg PA
CBHW071518080526
44588CB00011B/1474